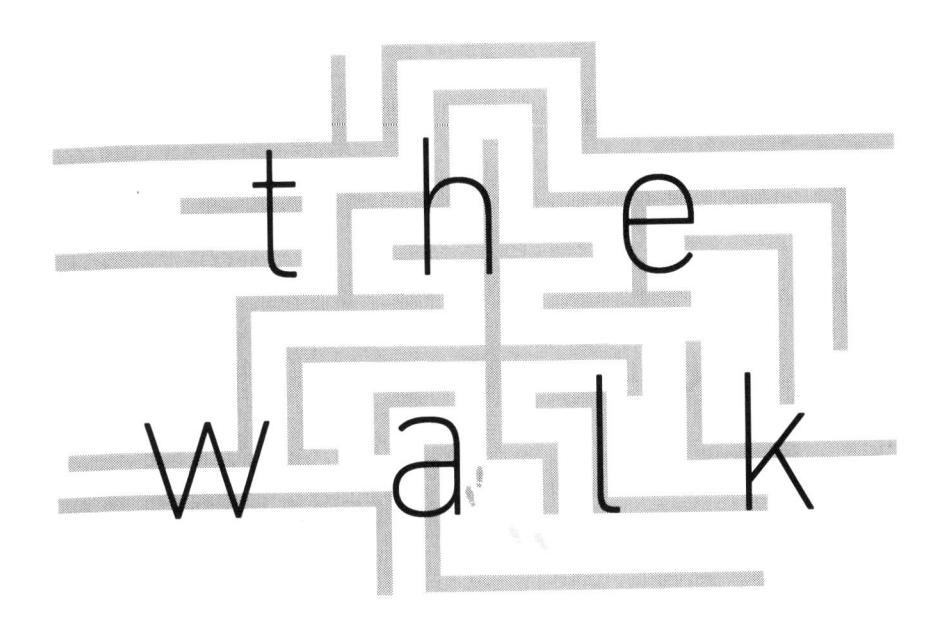

the walk

Love

Denny & Karri
  Allen

Phil 4:13

DENNY + KARRI
ALLEN

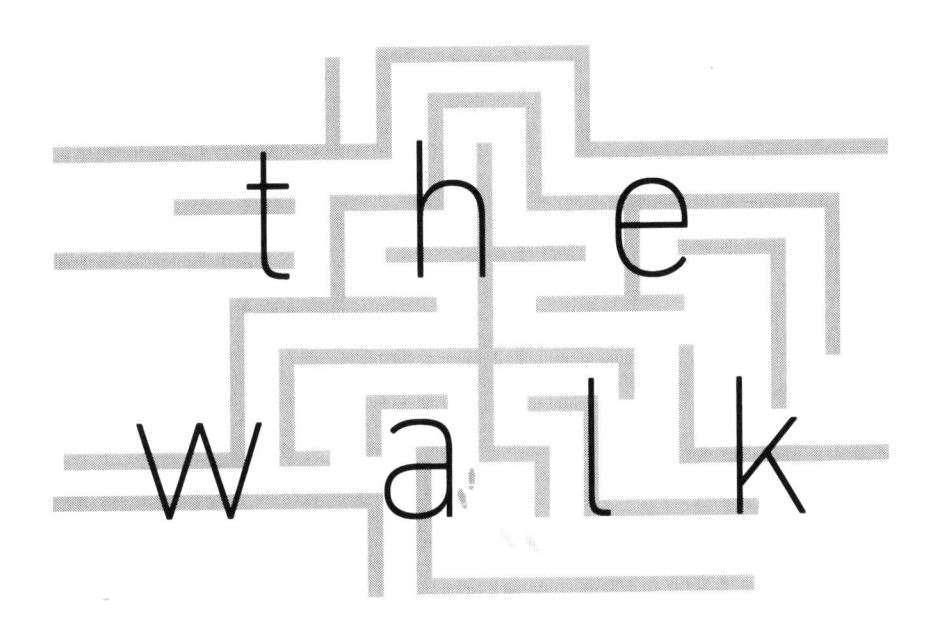

the walk

OUR STORY OF HOPE, HEALING +
HOW TO HELP
A LOVED ONE WHO HAS LOST A CHILD

THRONE
PUBLISHING GROUP

Copyright © 2017 by Denny and Karri Allen

ISBN: 978-1-945255-51-9

All rights reserved. No part of this book may be reproduced or transmitted in any form or by any means, electronic or mechanical, including photocopying, recording or by any information storage and retrieval system, without permission in writing from the copyright owner. For information on distribution rights, royalties, derivative works or licensing opportunities on behalf of this content or work, please contact the publisher at the address below.

Printed in the United States of America.

Although the author and publisher have made every effort to ensure that the information and advice in this book was correct and accurate at press time, the author and publisher do not assume and hereby disclaim any liability to any party for any loss, damage, or disruption caused from acting upon the information in this book or by errors or omissions, whether such errors or omissions result from negligence, accident, or any other cause.

Throne Publishing Group
2329 N Career Ave #215
Sioux Falls, SD 57107
ThronePG.com

table of contents

Introduction — vii

part one: our story

1. Our Boy — 3
2. Our Heartbreak — 11

part two: our walk

3. Our Decision — 25
4. Our Hope — 33

part three: our support

5. The X Factor — 45
6. The Immediate — 57
7. Ongoing — 69

Conclusion: The Walk — 81

About the Authors — 83

About Healing Hope Ministries — 85

introduction

Thank you for picking up this book. By doing so, you have taken the first bold step toward walking the journey with parents whose child has died. We wrote this book not because we have all of the answers, but because we want to walk alongside you during this journey. We are a resource for you and your family, and we want to be here when you need us.

There are no stupid questions. There is no feeling that you can feel that you should be afraid to share with us. If it's humanly possible to feel anger, joy, despair, confusion, and pain all in the same moment, then that's what it feels like to feel loss. Don't fear or try to rationalize the emotions—simply accept them and be willing to take each step in the walk as it comes.

Through this book, we'll touch on important events from our own story to help guide you through yours. We'll also share tips and insights for things you can say and do to help the loved ones in your life begin to heal.

Thank you for seeking advice, and thank you for trusting us. We're here for you. You can do this.

—*Denny & Karri Allen, July 2017*

part one

our story

1
our boy

I've always liked beginnings, and I believe that the way you begin a journey is just as important as the way that you end it. My walk with Denny began with a strong connection. And even though our path has gone through many twists and turns during our journey, we made a commitment to keep the connection strong. We have never lost sight of each other, and we never plan to.

Where It All Started

Denny and I first met at the South Dakota School of Massage Therapy. Both of us were taking classes there to fulfill the shared dream of a new career. Denny had just returned from Iraq, and during introductions on the first day, we realized a funny connection. He and my brother-in-law had been deployed together in the Army National Guard!

the walk

We became close friends after that, studying, hanging out, and talking together until 2:00 or 3:00 a.m. But Denny still wouldn't ask me out. He was a recovering alcoholic who was 13 years older than me and had given up on the idea of ever getting married. Finally, his sister Connie asked, "Why don't you just date her already?" and something clicked. So we dated for a few months and on December 4, 2008, Denny proposed. We set the wedding date for March 28, 2009. It was only three months away, but we wanted to get married before Denny's next deployment.

Three weeks after the wedding, Denny was deployed again. We spent the first year of our marriage thousands of miles apart.

In Comes Asher

When we found out we were pregnant with our first child in July 2010, I was overjoyed. As soon as I saw the "positive" on the test, I ran back to bed shouting, "I'm pregnant!" I had wanted to be a mom for a long time, and I couldn't wait to start the journey with Denny.

Denny was excited, too, though a little uneasy at the same time. He was 41 years old, which he thought was a little older than a new father should be. He had left his job as a phone technician to attend massage therapy school, and he wasn't sure how he would provide for our family. He also suffered from post-traumatic stress disorder (PTSD) that had hit after the death of four friends in Iraq, and the death of his mother the year before.

Denny had also become a father early in life, at age 21, and had not made a lot of good choices at that time. He wanted to show that he had become a better man, and that he could do it right this time. So he committed and refocused, and went into "provider mode". He set aside his dreams of being a massage therapist and got his job back as a phone technician. Neither of us could wait to welcome the beautiful baby boy who was about to enter our lives.

The pregnancy was easier than I thought it would be. It was even fun, especially since my sister was pregnant at the same time. The only downsides were that I couldn't handle the smell of coffee, and the baby also didn't seem to want to come out. "I just want my baby!" was something I said a lot near the end of the nine months. Finally, nine days past my due date, we induced. It took 52 hours of labor, but it was all worth it. We met our beautiful, healthy baby boy on March 25, one of the best days of my life.

We named our boy Asher, which means "happy" or "blessed"—and he lived up to his name. He was a giggly, joyful baby who hardly ever screamed or cried. He loved baths and playing outside, although he would get mad and hold his breath if you took away the stick he was playing with. Asher loved to dance and bounce to music, especially to the praise band at church. He had fiery red hair and a peaceful presence that inspired everyone around him.

Our laughter-filled little boy brought love, healing, and a renewed sense of purpose—especially to Denny. In his role as Asher's father, Denny learned that a family could be a strong, unified force. Fatherhood was a thing to be treasured, not feared. For the first time, Denny began to identify family with a sense of joy.

the walk

Milestones and Memories

Like many proud parents, we loved going through Asher's firsts. He had a beautiful baptism and, a couple months later, he rolled over and began crawling. He took his first steps right before his first Christmas. His bright red hair, beautiful blue eyes, and joyous nature made for many picture-perfect occasions we still cherish today.

In the evenings, Denny would turn on Mickey Mouse and Asher would stop what he was doing, turn around, look at the TV, and back right into Denny's lap. Together, the two of them would watch, snuggle, and laugh until bedtime. Then Asher would get up and walk to bed, dragging his blanket behind him without a fuss. It was, like so many things this blessed little boy did, unique.

Asher also had a unique way of letting us know that he was awake in the mornings. He would simply lift up his legs and thump them on the crib mattress. No screaming or crying for little Asher—just *thump*, and then again, *thump*.

Asher's first birthday was another unique and special occasion. We decided to host a Mickey Mouse-themed bash and invite lots of people. On the day of the party, our house was filled with more than 50 friends and family members.

Asher thought his Mickey Mouse onesie and Mickey Mouse balloons were the coolest things in the world. He even snuck off at one point to open one of his gifts before he was supposed to. It was a little stuffed Mickey Mouse—a special keepsake for us to this day. And, as with many one-year-olds, Asher ended up wearing more of his birthday cake than he ate.

We kept wondering why we had decided to host such a large party, especially since Denny's PTSD made it hard for him to be around crowds. But today, we know it was meant to be. To this day, we are grateful that we made the most of Asher's first birthday, since it was the only one we would get to spend with our sweet little boy.

2
our heartbreak

Monday, July 2, 2012: The Day Asher Went to Heaven

It started like any other Monday. Denny woke up at 5:30 a.m., got ready, and headed to work just as he always did. Around 10:00 a.m., he stopped back home for a coffee break since the place he worked was just down the street. He met me in the living room, and we both noticed that Asher seemed a little more tired than usual. But we'd had a very busy weekend, and figured he was simply tired. Denny returned to work and we went about the rest of our morning.

Since Asher seemed tired, I fed him his lunch early and put him down for his nap around 11:20 a.m. But something seemed *off* to me, and I stayed outside the doorway of his room, listening as he cried himself to sleep. All of a sudden, Asher went completely silent… and I knew in my gut that something was deeply wrong. I hurried back into his room and found him hunched over in the corner of his crib. I lifted him up, and felt that his body was limp.

With an increasing sense of fear and dread, I called Denny. I said, "I think there's something wrong with Asher." He left work immediately and was at our doorstep in minutes. "Just call," he said upon seeing Asher, and I dialed 911.

It felt like total chaos as fire trucks, police, and an ambulance arrived. They loaded Asher into the back of the ambulance, strapped me in the front, and raced for the hospital. Denny followed us in the minivan, and called his sister Connie to tell her we were taking Asher to the hospital. He stopped only once as the ambulance came to a sudden halt on a busy street.

Denny didn't know what was going on or why the ambulance had stopped. But at that moment, despite the hellish pain and terror, he felt the unmistakable presence of God. It only lasted for a brief second before the terror returned, like the spot of calm in the eye of a storm. But he knew then, without a doubt, what the outcome of the day would be.

In his mind, the words of the Lord echoed: *I have Asher.*

Instantly, the panic returned, and brought with it anger and disbelief. It sounds reassuring now, that the Lord had Asher, but at the time, as a parent, it was not a good thing. We didn't want the Lord to have Asher yet. We weren't ready to let him go. If God had a plan, it was a plan we didn't want.

Denny didn't tell me about this part until much later. I was in so much denial that I don't know if I would have believed him, heard him, or understood the words.

Meanwhile, in the stopped ambulance, I was twisting against the restraints of my seat, trying to see into the back. I was trying to figure out why it had stopped. I later learned that the paramedics were having a hard time getting an IV started. In a last-ditch effort, they had stopped the ambulance to insert the IV into one of Asher's legs.

We reached the hospital, where we waited anxiously in a small room while Asher was wheeled into the ER. Denny's sister Connie arrived with her husband, and we were so grateful to have them there with us.

Asher was in the ER for what felt like forever, even though it was probably only 30 minutes. When a doctor finally came to talk to us, all I could do was listen for the words, "He's okay."

But they never came.

Instead, the room seemed to darken and close in on us as the doctor said the most devastating words a parent can hear: "We lost him. He didn't make it."

Hearing the Words

Heaviness, dread, and complete sickness crashed down instantly upon our hearts. Denny stood still, though I wanted to rush toward the observation room where Asher was being kept. I wanted to be in there with him. I couldn't believe he was not okay, that I couldn't fix what was wrong with my baby boy. I thought that if I could just touch him, he would wake up.

the walk

Connie was there with us when we heard the news, and took on the task of telling the rest of the family what had happened. Soon, a lot of people had crowded into the room with us. We were grateful for them, and grateful that Connie had found the words to tell them. We had not known what to say—it didn't feel like there were words to convey the terrible message.

Then, minutes later, a police officer separated and questioned us. It wasn't intended to be cruel—we were told that it's standard procedure when a child dies. And our police officer was sympathetic. He had a sister who had lost a child, so there was empathy and a blessing there. He even gave us some helpful resources.

But even though we knew the police officer was only doing his job, the process was still painful and upsetting. In a daze, we described our morning, explaining events that did not yet seem real.

"How did your son get that bruise on his leg?" the police officer asked Denny, referring to the mark where the paramedics had put the IV into Asher's leg. Denny didn't know—he hadn't been in the ambulance.

"Would your wife have any reason to do this?" was the next question. Again, it was a standard question, and the police officer wasn't blaming us. The pain was real for him, too. He had been there to see our son's dead body.

"Did you shake your baby?" the police officer asked when he questioned me. And even though I hadn't, I began to wonder—had I done something wrong? Grief and shock met the lingering question and spiraled into a sense of guilt that deepened the wound in my heart. *They're trying to blame me for this*, I thought. And then, *What if I hurt Asher and didn't know it? What if they send me to jail? What if it is my fault?*

We never did receive an explanation for why Asher had died. Even to this day, it remains a mystery. His autopsy results came back completely normal.

The Empty Car Seat

The next impossible step was leaving the hospital. Somehow, Denny and I both knew in our hearts that once we walked out of those doors, the whole ordeal would be final. We would have to acknowledge that our son was dead and gone, and we wouldn't see him again until the funeral. And we weren't ready to do that yet. So we kept coming up with reasons not to leave. Finally, we had to admit that we couldn't stay in the hospital forever.

Every step toward the door brought us closer and closer to a reality that we were not prepared to face. One of Denny's cousins had volunteered to drive us home, and we walked out to the van with him. Denny sat in the front with him, and I sat in the back, next to Asher's now-empty car seat, with his blanket in my hand.

When we arrived home, Denny's cousin wasn't sure what to do, so he asked if we would like him to stay with us or leave us alone. I was still in shock, but I remember feeling grateful that he had thought to ask. I told him that I wanted him to stay, and he did.

I don't have the words for what it was like to walk into the house. Only hours before, our house had been the home to our joyful little family. Now it was empty, dark, and silent. Asher's lunch was still out on the high chair. His toys were all over the floor. There were reminders everywhere that he had just been there—and now he simply wasn't. It was the heaviest feeling in the world.

Soon our friends, family, and coworkers started to arrive, which helped the house to feel a little less desolate. But despite the number of people, there was still a lot of silence. There were a lot of hugs and tears and togetherness, too, but mostly there was silence. Still, these wonderful people were there for us, letting us know that despite how awful we felt, we were not alone.

The First Night of Silence

That afternoon, there were people everywhere. We had a constant stream of loved ones coming and going. We felt protected, like we had some padding between us and the pain. But when night fell, most of the guests left and it was like the physical support dropped away. Reality slammed in and I began to scream and cry, my whole body shaking.

Denny said later that I was crying so violently it was like I was having seizures in bed. My whole body was engaged in processing the pain of the day. My mother and two of my sisters joined us in bed and just held me. No one was sure what to do, but being together helped.

There was physical pain, too, in addition to our spiritual and emotional pain. Our tense muscles would not relax, our hearts literally ached, and we were left gasping for breath. We discovered that grief and loss make for an intense, whole-body experience.

No one in the house slept that night—the family that remained with us watched the clock slowly tick, time passing second by second. The questions the police officer had asked kept racing through my mind, spurred on by grief and shock: *Did you shake your baby? What if they send me to jail? What if it is my fault?*

You see, Satan had planted a seed of doubt in my heart. So while I knew the questions weren't true, they were still rooted in the doubt within my heart, wounding me further.

The Next Few Days

The next few days were clouded by crying, disbelief, and complete uncertainty. As we sorted through pictures, reminiscing and trying to make funeral arrangements, the funeral director asked where Asher was going to be buried. Of course we hadn't made such plans for our healthy baby boy.

Thankfully, my mother was there to help. My father had passed away the previous April, and she lovingly suggested that Asher could be buried next to his Grandpa. This suggestion removed a huge burden that we hadn't even realized was there.

In the days before the funeral, the steady stream of loving and supporting visitors (and food) did not stop. People wanted to help—in fact, they seemed desperate to help. We had first thought there was nothing anyone could do to ease our pain, but soon realized something. Even seeing familiar faces walking through the door (no matter if they were friend, family, or coworker) was comforting. We were grateful for each and every person who took that bold step through our door into the unknown with us.

The house was active—our visitors were eager to help cook and clean, as though action could somehow help remove the immense feeling of shock and loss. Busy chatter and nervous conversation filled the air.

Every time a new person entered the house, we would tell them the story. And in doing that, we would relive it all, get hit by the weight of losing Asher, and then settle back into numbness. It happened again and again, hundreds of times even in the first 48 hours. Looking back, there was healing in this. But at the time, it was not fun.

The Funeral

On the day of the funeral, I remember waking up first thinking that it was all a bad dream. My next thought was, "Can we not go through this today? Can we just go hide somewhere? Can't we just fly away?" Attending the funeral would mean admitting one final time that Asher had died. It was still not something Denny or I wanted to admit.

Reality set in as we looked over the funeral clothes we had laid out the night before, and answered texts about funeral plans. Thankfully, our families were there to help us carry out that plan whether or not we had the mental, emotional, or physical strength to do so. We *had* to march through the steps, whether we wanted to or not. It was real, and it was happening.

The funeral was held in our home church, and when we arrived to view Asher, we were struck by how tiny he was—how little his casket was. The casket was so small, it fit on a table, surrounded by his baby books and several favorite toys. It was so small, it looked *wrong* somehow. It was heartbreaking.

Then people began to flood in for the viewing—a steady stream for two hours. With every person we greeted, we felt a weight on our shoulders, and then a release, over and over for two exhausting hours.

We had planned the funeral to not only honor Asher's life, but bring people to Christ. And although we had carefully selected the music and lessons, the service itself felt surreal. It felt as though we were watching a movie or floating through a dream, disconnected from reality. Denny told me later that more than once, he found himself thinking, "This isn't real."

After the service and a luncheon, we invited everyone to join us for the drive to the gravesite, which was two hours away. Since the casket was so small, the funeral director asked us if we wanted Asher to ride with us in our van. We said yes, and the best man from our wedding offered to drive us, so Denny and I sat in the back of the van for one last family outing.

We spent most of the drive watching the slideshow we had put together for the funeral. "I loved it," Denny told me later. "It was powerful, having him with us. It was my boy and his life."

the walk

When we arrived at the cemetery, neither of us wanted to leave the car. We wanted to hold on to that moment for as long as possible. It was heartbreaking to have Asher in the casket, but at least the three of us were together. We did not want to put him in the ground. But it was part of the path we had to walk, and so we walked it.

The burial took place on July 6, 2012. It felt like the hottest day on record, especially since the cemetery had no shade. Denny spent a lot of the time worrying about his father's poor health in the heat, though soon felt an overwhelming sense of peace. He realized that the funeral had really happened, and that Asher was with God. It was not a lasting feeling—a recurring sense of denial would set in again days, weeks, and months later—but at the time, it was enough.

part two

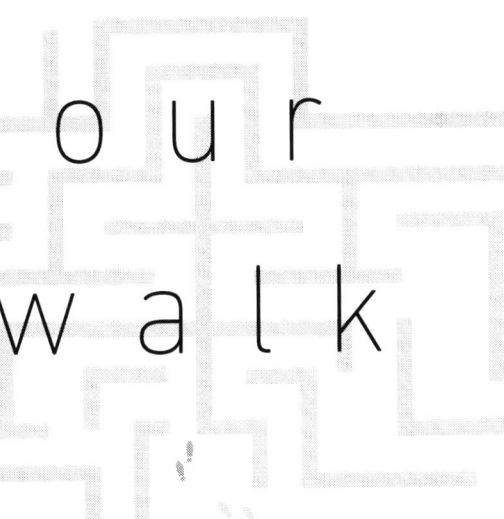

our walk

3
our decision

The Shared Brokenness

You may have heard that 88% of marriages end in divorce after a child dies. When Asher died, Denny and I didn't want to be just another statistic. But we had no idea how hard it would be to hold our marriage together. Without the help, strength, and support of our friends and family, I don't think we would have been able to.

It almost doesn't make sense. After the death of a child, you'd think that a husband and wife would need each other more than ever before. After all, they share a grief and a brokenness that few other people can really understand.

Our experience with Asher helped us to understand why the divorce statistic is so high. Imagine that you've broken your right leg, and you need a pair of crutches to get around. The crutches work because your left leg is strong enough to guide and support your broken right leg. You can manage the loss because the whole system is not broken. There is still one steady leg to lean on.

But if both of your legs are broken, those crutches won't do you any good.

The death of a parent for the married couple is like using crutches with one broken leg. The pain is great, but not equally great for both the husband and wife. So one can stand as a steady rock or anchor for the other.

For example, my dad died in 2011. Denny loved him, but had been deployed to Kuwait for half of our two-year-old marriage. He didn't have more than 20 years of memories with my dad like I did. So while his death was painful, Denny wasn't stuck with me in the pit of despair. He was equipped and able to stay strong for me through that loss. He could help guide me through it.

But the death of a child is like using crutches with two broken legs. When Asher died, we were both equally attached to him. He was *our* son. The heartbreak was distinct and terrible and it hit us equally hard. We were both drowning in that pit of despair, and we couldn't pull each other out.

We needed someone to pull us out. We needed someone to lean on or our marriage would crumble.

For us, the help came from God, our family, and our friends. We are forever grateful for the loving and wonderful network of support they gave us. It saved our marriage and it is one of the reasons we decided to write this book.

Grief Shared Among Us

When a child dies, you become part of a close-knit network of people who have been through a similar loss. During the funeral, we were approached by several couples who looked us in the eye and said simply, "We've been through this."

That one simple phrase said so much, especially with the eye contact and other nonverbal cues. It said, *You're not alone—this happens to other people.* It said, *You can get through this.* It said, *You're going to make it. See? We're still standing, and you will be, too.*

And we heard it from people we hadn't even *known* had lost a child. Couples in their 50s and 60s we had known for years, young couples whom we hadn't known were ever pregnant. They didn't tell us what to think or how to feel, but the compassion and shared grief in their eyes planted a small seed of hope.

The Beginning of True Grief

Sometime during the first night—hours after Asher had died—Denny disappeared.

Our house was still full of friends, family, coworkers, and other people sharing our grief. So I went from room to room, looking for Denny and asking if anyone had seen him. But no one had seen him for a while. No one knew where he had gone.

the walk

I was starting to get worried, so I checked the bedroom a second time. It was then that I saw Denny, kneeling on the floor beside the bed, clinging to his Bible. He was in bad shape. He had already been through so much in his life: incredible loss, PTSD from Iraq, suicidal thoughts, his own alcoholism—and now his baby was dead.

Denny was at the end of his rope. He couldn't take any more. Nothing mattered to him, and he felt like nothing would ever matter again. At that point, he wanted to die.

Denny had gone through a lot at a young age, and suicide was never far from his thoughts. Though he had never made an actual plan for it, it always felt like an option if things got bad enough. Had God not intervened, I very well could have lost my husband, as well.

I entered the room and knelt down beside my husband. Our marriage hadn't been perfect before Asher's death. It was far from perfect now. It was probably already on its way to becoming a statistic. But I made the choice to join Denny and kneel beside him, and in that moment, a miracle happened.

Denny later told me that while he was on his knees, clinging to his Bible, he had heard the voice of God. "There are a couple ways you can do this, son," the voice said. "You can run toward me—and I mean *run*, not walk or crawl—or you can run away from me."

When Denny looked up, he saw me kneeling beside him—he hadn't heard me come into the bedroom. But he was compelled to speak these words: "There are two ways we can go here," he told me. "We can either run toward God or away from Him. I know which way I'm going because I've got nothing left. Do you want to come with me?"

At that point, I didn't feel like I was ready to commit to anything, or to stop clinging to the hope that this was all a bad dream. It was just hours after Asher's death, and I was still caught up in the *why*. But I knew I wanted to go in that direction eventually, and I knew God would want us to turn this thing that had happened into something good.

So I said, "Okay."

It was a moment of acceptance for both of us. Acceptance that we had no strength on our own. Acceptance of whom we needed to go to for that strength. Acceptance of not *who* we were, but *whose* we were.

Denny later told me that the words he spoke that night were not his own. The strength was not his, either. It was the inspired word and strength of God. We received a miracle that night while we were on our knees together.

It wasn't a miracle of immediate healing or the removal of our grief, though. It wasn't a miracle of Asher coming back to life. It was the humble planting of a seed. It was the beginning of God's strength pouring into our lives, the beginning of His carrying us through everything.

God drew us there together to make a choice. It wasn't something anyone else could do for us. We had to choose to go through this together, as a unified couple. We had to choose to lean on the strength and might of a God who loved us. We had to choose to put our marriage in His hands and trust Him to guide us through the door.

Choice Becomes Divine Appointment

No matter how bad things may seem, we always have a choice. You can't choose what happens to you in life, but you can choose how you respond to it.

That night, God presented us with a choice. He did not make the choice for us—only we could do that. Only we could reach out and take the divine hand that was being extended to us. Only we could choose to accept God's divine appointment as a unified couple.

Our favorite Bible verse is Philippians 4:13: *"I can do all things through Christ who strengthens me."* God always wants to give strength, power, and love to you. But you have to choose to let Him into your life. You have to choose to accept it. You have to realize you can't do it all yourself.

And things weren't perfect for us, even after we made that choice. Asher was still gone, and both Denny and I had years of painful grief and healing ahead of us. After the death of a child, parents are considered "newly bereaved" for up to *five to seven years.*

But Denny and I were no longer trying to move forward on two broken legs. We had chosen to invite a loving and all-powerful God into our lives and our marriage. We were a couple united in faith.

4
our hope

Unified Yet Unique

One thing we learned in the months after Asher's death is that grief is complex and unique, and not everyone deals with it in the same way. And that's okay. As with anything in life, there are many paths that can lead to the same destination.

Many couples expect that they will travel the same path of grief together, side by side. But it's not a realistic expectation. If one spouse expects, insists, or forces the other to walk a path that's not right for them, things won't end well. The walk will end in bitterness, impatience, a lesser degree of healing, resentment, blame, and possibly divorce.

No one will grieve exactly the same way you do, but it's easy to want someone on that path with you at all times. It's also easy to assume that if another person is grieving *differently*, he or she is grieving *wrong*. This is especially easy to do if you don't fully understand the other person's style of grief.

People are complex. We all come from different places and different situations, and we all have different needs. Men and women are inherently different, too—Denny couldn't know what it was like to be a grieving mother. And I couldn't know what it was like to be a grieving father. But we were both equally hurting and grieving.

In the observation room moments after learning Asher had died, all I wanted to do was hold his body and caress his face. But Denny was hesitant. He didn't want to touch Asher or even be in the same room as his body. He wanted to be alone.

Later, I found that I wanted to talk about Asher a lot. I wanted to look at pictures of him and surround myself with the comfort of family and friends during my grief. I found myself especially drawn to other moms who had lost children. We'd talk and have lunch together for hours. But Denny preferred to be secluded. He threw himself into his work and spent hours alone in the evenings, watching sermons on TV.

At the time, I wanted him to look at pictures of Asher with me, or be present with friends and family. I wanted him to grieve beside me on my path, and it was frustrating that he wasn't there.

It was easy to make assumptions. I could see that Denny was isolating himself, and it was easy (and logical) to assume that he had withdrawn. It was easy to assume that he didn't want to spend time with me and help me through my grief. It was easy to assume that he was *doing it wrong*.

I learned later that Denny had been thinking the same thing about me! He wanted me to watch those healing sermons with him and be hungry for God's truth in the same way he was. He saw me surrounded by family and friends, and he felt isolated and jealous.

It was easy for him to assume that no one cared about him. It was easy for him to assume that I didn't care to travel the path of healing with him in his way. It was easy for him to assume that I was *doing it wrong*.

These assumptions made us feel hurt, bitter, and resentful toward each other. They kept us right where Satan wanted us, in a place of weakness, chaos, and misunderstanding. It felt like our marriage was under attack.

I think we were also frustrated or disappointed that we couldn't heal each other. Denny and I are both very giving people, and wanted to be everything for each other. But that simply did not (and could not) happen. We needed healing directly from the source.

Denny got God's truth directly from the pastors' sermons on TV. I got love, truth, and nurturing poured into me from the women in my life. Denny and I both had faith, but we also had to give each other grace to walk the path according to our needs. While we didn't see it at the time, our different paths were leading us to the same place.

Grief is different for everyone, so be very careful not to assume you know what someone else is feeling. And do not assume that what you view on the *outside* is what's going on *inside*. Just because someone turns inward or withdraws from society doesn't mean they don't care. And just because someone turns to family and friends doesn't mean they don't need *you*.

Walk in faith and extend grace to each other, and know that different paths can lead to the same healing.

That July and August, Denny and I each made another decision about where our paths would go. Denny kept pouring himself into the Word. One of the HR ladies at his workplace had rallied others to donate vacation time to help cover his salary so he didn't miss a paycheck. It was a huge blessing.

For my part, I decided to continue going to my MOPS group. MOPS stands for "Mothers of Preschoolers" and it's a Christian group that meets twice a month to celebrate the joys and struggles of raising children. The kids often attend with their moms. I had attended the previous year with Asher and made several good friends. It was starting up again the first weekend in September, and I decided to attend even though Asher (my only child at the time) had died.

In that first meeting, I shared my story right away so that all of the new women who had joined that year wouldn't feel awkward around me when they'd ask, "So, how many kids do you have?" or avoid the subject of kids altogether. I didn't want anyone to feel uncomfortable in any way. "I'm still a mom," I explained. "I still have a child like you do. I just can't see him right now."

There is a yearly theme for MOPS, and that year our theme was "Plunge: love as if your life depended on it". It was such a blessing to be able to share Asher's story surrounded by loving, supporting moms who were willing to take the plunge with me and go deep.

Lives were touched and changed, and Denny and I began to move forward into our "new normal".

Our Retreat

Denny found the retreat center out of desperation. He was searching online to see if there was any hope for our marriage. Even though we had made the decision to let God guide our grief, it was still incredibly difficult.

God stirred in him the desire to take action and seek help, and he soon found Smile Again Ministries in northern Minnesota. He presented the idea to me and immediately I knew we needed to do it. We made the decision quickly—Denny found the retreat center one afternoon in September and lined everything up that day.

I've never been much of a talker with Denny, and some folks who know me might call me reserved or even stoic. So a retreat that focused on meaningful conversation and opening up was exactly what we needed. Smile Again Ministries also keeps things small. Their retreats involve just one or two couples instead of several dozen, which again was just what we needed.

Everything fell into place, and we left for our retreat in October 2012, just three months after Asher had died. But even though everything fell into place perfectly, it wasn't an easy trip.

Smile Again Ministries is pretty far off the grid, and it wasn't findable by GPS. It was literally in the middle of nowhere. The road that led to the retreat center was no more than a soft dirt trail surrounded by trees.

The lane finally ended and we pulled up to a beautiful sign and a log cabin-style lodge, and instantly felt a sense of tranquility and peace. It was as though we had entered into a safe, loving place, and we could breathe again.

Smile Again Ministries is run by Pat and Judy Misener, who lost their 13-year old daughter Mickey to heart disease in 1988. They now devote their lives to ministering and counseling grieving parents, helping them to find hope and peace in their pain.

Pat and Judy welcomed us warmly and immediately showered us with love. They taught us grieving and healing techniques, and new ways of thinking that helped strengthen our marriage.

Pat and Judy also helped us fully understand the scope of what we were up against. They informed us of the risks to our marriage, and let us know what would come between us so that we could prepare and invest in our relationship. With their help, we learned how to grow and strengthen our marriage. They were the ones who taught us that men and women grieve differently, and assured us that it was okay. They also told us that American society tends to assume that a father's grief is less than a mother's. Because of that, fathers have a much more limited support network than mothers. The Miseners were looking to change that.

They also told us that after the first year following the death of a child, society would expect us to "get over it" and "move on". They were honest with us about the second year possibly being harder than the first. They prepared us well for the hard road ahead and gave us hope because their marriage was so strong.

We learned about the different stages and emotions of grief, and Pat and Judy helped us figure out where we were on the path toward healing. They outlined the steps we would need to take to come out where they were on the other side. We learned that we still had a lot of work to do, and a long way to go.

It was also hard for us to hear that we had to take the steps forward ourselves—that no one could do it for us. Our friends and family (and Pat and Judy, too) were there to help us and encourage us, but *only we could choose to take the steps*. Only we could open the doors and walk through them.

Our retreat with Smile Again Ministries was life-changing, and quite possibly life-saving. It forced us to sit in our grief for days and get comfortable focusing on it. It gave us a healthy dose of our present reality and hope for the future. It also granted us a vision of how good our marriage could be.

We want to be very clear that when we left the retreat, we were not fully healed by any means. But we were different. Our eyes had been opened and our hearts had been changed. Pat and Judy are one of the main reasons we decided to start Healing Hope Ministries and bring a healing retreat experience to South Dakota.

Home Again

Going to the retreat didn't fix everything and it didn't magically heal us. Things weren't perfect when we got home, either. Some things had popped up during the retreat that had really scared me. It had also forced us to talk about other issues with our marriage that had been a problem even before Asher died.

In addition to that, our initial shock had begun to wear off and our grief was becoming more clarified. We were scared how close we still were to the beginning of the grieving process. We had hope, but we also knew we had a lot of pain ahead of us.

During our retreat, Pat and Judy were adamant that we continue to go to counseling on a weekly basis. It was a total "God thing" that we returned from the retreat on Sunday and had a session scheduled that Monday. We were in rough shape.

During our session, we talked to the counselor about our retreat. We were able to expand on and walk through some of the issues that had arisen there. We also learned that while we were moving slowly, at least we were moving forward.

The counselor affirmed what we'd learned during our retreat. He also told us that even though Denny and I were walking different paths of grief, we needed to stay within sight of each other. It's easy to want to sprint ahead and just get the pain over with. But if I were to get too far ahead of Denny, I would lose sight of his needs and he would lose sight of mine.

So even though we wanted to be five feet from the finish line, we had to commit to keeping pace with each other. We needed to be unified, patient, and gracious to each other. And while it's not easy, it *is* worth it.

part three

our support

5
the x factor

You Mean the World: the Family Unit

As you have seen so far throughout the book, the family unit has an amazing impact on the healing process. What do we mean by "family unit"? We're talking about:

- Immediate family members
- Other close family members
- Close friends
- Close coworkers
- Other individuals who have walked a similar path of loss

Not everyone in the family unit needs to be related by blood. In fact, there could be very few actual family members in the family unit. And that's okay.

the walk

No matter who makes up the family unit, it is crucial for many reasons. First and foremost, with loss comes change. For instance, before the death of a child, a father might have been the biggest Vikings fan in the world. But after the loss, he might be completely disinterested in football. Everything has changed for him, including his priorities, his hobbies, and possibly even the person he will become.

As a member of the family unit, chances are, you were there before the loss. You know the couple's starting point and identity. You know what their hopes and dreams had been. You know who they wanted to become. You also need to be accepting of change. The father might never be interested in football again, and that is okay. His football buddies may not understand, or may feel rejected, which is why he needs you (and the rest of the family unit) even more. Your role is to stand beside them, helping them to make good choices and reminding them that they are loved.

After Asher died, our circle of friends changed. Some of the people we had considered close friends couldn't relate to or handle our loss. They didn't know how to act around us and we didn't really know how to move forward.

After Asher's death, there were days when I didn't think I had the strength to get out of bed. But those were the days when members of our family unit showed up and gave me the boost I needed to get going.

There were days when Denny and I felt like we were drowning in sorrow and despair, and on those days our family unit kept us above water. There was always someone there for us. We were only able to get through the moments, days, weeks, and months because of their support. They did not question or judge us. They were simply there, loving us through it all.

By being there, they also helped us remember that we were not alone. On the days following Asher's death, members of our family unit took care of the house, helped plan the funeral, and brought food. They even kept track of who had dropped off different items so we could thank them after it was all over.

The family unit is there to listen, hug, cook, and clean. The family unit can help the couple remember fond memories, observe special dates, and even say the child's name aloud. These are all crucial for healing, even though they might seem small or simple at the time.

People may change during and after a loss—often for good. At their core, they will remain the same person. But they may shift priorities, behave differently, or lose interest in superficial things. What they need from you during this time is your steadfast love, presence, and acceptance.

Understand Where They Are

As a member of the family unit, the first step in helping someone you love is to make the effort to understand where they are. And the first step in understanding is getting rid of fear.

Fear

Loss is scary, and not just for the couple whose child has died. It's scary for everyone. It's painful, it raises the possibility that it could happen to anyone.

That was one thing we learned when Asher died. People wanted to help us, but they were scared that they would make a mistake and cause us further pain. Because of that, many of them stayed away or avoided us during our time of grief. They told themselves they wanted to respect our privacy, or that they didn't want to intrude.

But we wanted them there. We needed them there. We were drowning and we needed our family unit to be strong for us and surround us with love. The rest of this book will give you ideas on what to do and say so that you can be there for the ones you love without the fear of messing anything up.

One of the biggest things you can do to get rid of fear is to step into the lives of the couple. Embrace them and embrace where they are. They are going to be feeling a huge range of emotions: denial, anger, guilt, hopelessness, fear, desperation, and enormous pain. Sometimes they will feel them all at once, and sometimes they will feel nothing at all. They might tell you they want to die, or that they don't care about anything anymore.

But don't be afraid. These feelings, while awful and unbearable, are somewhat normal. They can seem scary, and it can be hard for the family unit to see their loved ones in such pain. But this is their ground zero, and you can't change or take away those emotions.

You can't take away the pain or the hopelessness. You can't do anything to *fix* their lives.

What you *can* do is be there with them. You can decide not to let fear keep you away. You don't need counselor training or a degree in psychology. You don't even need to talk. Just show up. Be present. Walk into the pain and hopelessness, and even embrace it temporarily.

They may not say it at the time, but they will be grateful.

Assumptions

It's easy to feel fear, and it's also easy to make assumptions. It's easy to assume you know what it feels like to lose a child. Even if you have lost a child, everyone's grief is unique.

It's also easy to assume that someone else is stepping up to help. After Asher's death, I had one friend who assumed our house would be full of friends and family, and that she would simply be in the way if she came over. But she came over anyway, and it turned out that no one else was at our house yet. She was one of the first people to stop by our house after we got back home. She was a blessing.

Another assumption that many people make is that the couple can take care of themselves. But when you are in shock and grief, you don't know what you need. You don't have an appetite. You're not thinking about preparing meals or sleeping or washing the dishes. You are not even thinking about asking for help with any of these things.

So while the couple might be in survival mode, they might not be doing a great job of surviving. This is when they need you the most.

Observe, Ask, Act

As a member of the family unit, there are many ways you can help. After you get rid of the fear and assumptions in your heart, you can take three action steps: *observe, ask,* and *act.*

Observing means looking out for the couple and watching what's going on. Keep your eyes open for unmet needs:

- Have the grieving parents eaten yet today?
- Is the sink full of unwashed dishes?
- Are the beds made up for incoming guests?
- Are the bathrooms clean?
- Is there food in the house?
- Are the stairs and walkways covered in ice or snow?

Observe what's going on around you and then move on to the next step: ask. Once you've identified any unmet needs, ask the parents for permission to meet that need.

The way that you ask is important. Ask in a way that acknowledges the need and does not leave room for the parent to dismiss it. Ask in a way that will not burden or overwhelm the parent.

the x factor

If you ask, "Are you hungry?", the parent will probably say "No" because they are in shock and don't know that they're hungry. If you need to, clarify the unmet need with an easy yes or no question such as, "Have you eaten today?" If the parent says "No," ask permission to help them with a question like, "Can I bring you Subway?"

Other examples of questions include:

- "I'm going to bring you supper tonight. Is there a certain time you would like to eat?"
- "Can I pick up these toys?"
- "Can I wash these dishes?"
- "Can I make up some beds?"
- "Can I clean the bathroom?"
- "Can I go pick up some food for guests?"
- "Can I shovel the sidewalk?"
- "Can I mow the yard for you?"

Ask, "Can I do this for you?" and if you receive permission, act on it.

Acting is the third step, in which you fill the unmet needs you identified. If you have permission, then pick up the toys, wash the dishes, make up some meals to put in the freezer, mow the yard, and make up beds for guests. Think about their needs and be a step ahead of them.

None of this can happen if you are not present. Being present is one of the biggest blessings you can give the couple. Because while you can't take away their pain or fix their problems, you can help them move forward step by step.

So be bold. Walk through that door into their pain and hopelessness and grief. Don't be afraid and don't make assumptions. Instead, observe, ask, and act on any unmet needs.

How Our Family Unit Helped

Our family unit was an incredible blessing during our time of grief. They showed up to walk alongside us, embraced us where we were, and showered us with love.

After Asher died, several people in our family unit provided great examples of effective ways you can help grieving parents.

The first is Christina, a mother of two (at the time) who I met in my MOPS group ten months before Asher's death. We hadn't known each other long and she wasn't a member of my immediate family, so she hesitated to get in touch with us when she first heard about Asher's death. She didn't want to intrude where she felt she might not belong, since she was certain our house would be flooded with friends and family.

But she reached out to us anyway. She called at 4:00 p.m. on the day Asher died, and after some conversation asked, "Have you eaten today?" When I realized I hadn't, she asked if she could bring me Subway. I said yes, and she soon arrived with food.

Christina was the friend I referred to earlier, one of the first people to arrive at our house. She didn't counsel us or try to heal

the x factor

our pain. After she arrived with a platter of sandwiches from Subway, she stayed with us, and continued to observe, ask, and act. She asked if she could clean the kitchen for us. She asked if she could make beds and blow up air mattresses for our family as they began to arrive.

She was an absolute Godsend, an angel. Even though we weren't related and had only known each other a short time, she was a valuable member of our family unit.

Another example is my friend Bo. She called Denny right away when she heard about Asher and asked if she could set up a meal schedule for us. She called Denny because she didn't want me to have to deal with it, and made arrangements for a constant stream of food. She observed, asked, and acted. She was another Godsend and a member of our family unit during that time.

Not everyone—even members of the family unit—can be there right away because of travel, family situation, and other logistics. We understood that, and were grateful when our family members were able to arrive and be with us.

What surprised us most were the cards we got in the mail from people we didn't even know, people who had lost a child in our area. They sent us letters, little books, sayings, and prayer cards to encourage us. We read every single one, and they were so thoughtful and touching.

But even more than that, when I reached out to these people to thank them, it opened up the door to many new friendships. We added many new friends and new members of our family unit during that time.

the walk

As a member of the family unit, you are one of the most powerful forces in the couple's life, and are a crucial companion on their road to healing. Even if you aren't sure what to say or do, move past the fear and assumptions anyway. Reach out to the couple. Observe, ask, and act. It will mean the world to them.

6
the immediate

It's all about timing. We've already talked a little bit about things you can do to help, but in the next two chapters, we'll get more into what to say and do, and what *not* to say and do. We'll cover:

- The first 24 hours after the death up until the funeral,
- The funeral to the first three months after the death, and
- The ongoing grieving process, three months and on.

These are all practical things (dos and don'ts) that you can say and do to encourage the family and help them heal. You should come away from chapters six and seven with a good idea of how to take action to help the family.

The First 24 Hours to the Funeral

As we mentioned earlier, one of the most valuable things you can do immediately after a death is to simply *be present*. Be strong and commit to being in the moment with the family, accepting where they are, observing unmet needs, and acting on them.

We've talked with a lot of grieving parents, and found that many people say well-meaning but hurtful things after a death. Others try to cheer you up or fix the situation, which they can't do. So we've put together a list of helpful things you can say—and some *un*-helpful things you should try to avoid.

Things You Can Say:

- "I'm so sorry."
- "This is awful," or "This really sucks."
- "I wish I had the right words. Just know I care."
- "I am here to walk alongside you."
- "I am here for you."

Again, there are no magic words that will take away the pain. Just let the couple know that you are there with them, and that you love them.

Things to Avoid Saying:

- **"God has a plan,"** or **"It was God's will,"** or **"Everything happens for a reason."** These are clichés that minimize and dismiss the child's death. Also, do not presume to tell the parents what their belief system is. Everything has just been stripped away from them and thrown into question. They just buried their child. Even if you believe it was God's will, this is *not* the right time to tell the couple what to think or believe.
- **"God needed them more,"** or **"God needed another angel."** These words are often kindly meant, but not helpful.
- **"At least you have other kids,"** or **"You're young enough to have more kids."** Please do not say this. It comes off as extremely insensitive. No child can replace another child, and to assume so diminishes the child's memory.
- **"I know how you feel."** You can never truly know how another person feels in any situation. Do not presume to tell them or explain to them how they are feeling. Do not assume you know the depths of their grief or what happened in their life before this point.
- **"Be strong."** This may seem encouraging, but it comes off as one more impossible "to do" item for the couple to process and manage. It can also make them feel guilty or ashamed for feeling weak and broken. They are not going to be able to be strong for a long time.
- **"You guys are so strong,"** or **"You're handling this better than I expected."** This sends a mixed message to the couple, because the truth is they are *not* handling it. They are not being strong. Despite

what their appearance looks like, inside they are broken and barely able to stand. They are numb, in shock, and acting on autopilot.

- **"At least he died quickly,"** or **"At least he didn't suffer."** This is not helpful, and potentially not true. The child is still dead and gone—please do not try to find a silver lining for the parents.
- **"He's in a better place now."** This is also not helpful. To the parents, the best place their child could be is *with them*.
- **"How can I help you?"** or **"What do you need?"** The obvious answer to this question is, "I need my son back." Also, as we mentioned in chapter five, keep your questions specific and focused on unmet needs. The parents will not know what their needs are, and might feel helpless, guilty, or incompetent because of the question.

I hope this list doesn't scare you off from talking to the parents in a loving, helpful way. Please know that, to a point, words are just words. So when in doubt, trust your gut and show up. Just try to avoid pointing out a silver lining in the child's death.

Things You Can Do:

- **Show up.** Your presence is important. Take that bold step and walk through their door. If you can't be there in person, give them a call or send a handwritten card.
- **Give them a hug, sit with them, cry with them.** Be present in this time with the couple. Meet them where they are, and simply

the immediate

be yourself. If you need to cry, cry. If you need to hug them, hug them. Be as relevant, helpful, and present as you can.
- **Listen.** This is the most crucial thing you can do. Every thought and emotion you can imagine is spinning through the parents' minds, and they may need to talk to process their feelings. They will also need to tell the story. You don't need to respond or say the right words—just listen.
- **Talk about the child.** Many people will avoid talking about the child because they're afraid to further hurt the parents. But the parents need to hear that their child existed. They need to know that he was loved. They need to hear his name. They need to know he was real.
- **Offer to do something specific (observe, ask, act).** As we mentioned earlier, ask leading questions that are simple to answer. Guide them to the answer you know they need, and follow it up by asking permission and taking action.

Things Not to Do:

- **Do not pull out your Bible and start quoting Scripture.** Do not presume you know their religious beliefs or where they are with God right now. Do not tell them God has a plan. If they start the conversation about God and faith, listen more than you speak. They are possibly confused right now, but be patient with them. Pray with them and for them.

- **Do not give the parents a lecture or a sermon.** Now is not the time. They're not going to really hear you or process your words anyway.
- **Do not try to "fix it".** You cannot bring their child back. You cannot make anything "better" or cheer them up right now.
- **Do not assume the couple has a support system in place.** Many people are hesitant to "get in the way", and assume that the couple's house will be packed with family and close friends. But that may not be true. If everyone assumes that someone else is showing up, then no one shows up. If you feel like you should show up, show up.
- **Do not take offense at protective relatives.** It's natural for family members to go into protection mode. It doesn't mean that the couple doesn't want you there. So extend some grace to the grieving family members and be there for the couple regardless.

If you're uncertain of what to do, take a cue from the parents. If they want to talk about their child, they will. If they want to talk about the Bible, they will bring it up with you. If they want to cry, be present with them—and cry with them if you need to.

The Funeral to the First Three Months

Looking back, neither Denny nor I remember the funeral very well. We were still in shock, and it was all a blur—nothing that anyone said to us really registered. It may be difficult to believe or understand, but the parents' shock can last for several months.

Between the funeral and those first three months, Denny and I were still in shock. We were reluctant to "move on", even though the crowds of people disappeared from our house and it seemed like the rest of the world began to move on without us.

It was hard because we could still sense Asher in the house. This is very common for grieving parents. It's like an amputee who can still "feel" his missing leg. We thought we heard Asher laughing or thumping his legs in his crib to wake us up. In the evenings, we'd wait for him to run around the corner in the living room. We waited for months.

We also found it hard to leave our house. It had kind of turned into a safe bubble for us, a place of comfort where we were protected from reality. Going outside was scary and stressful. We never knew if we'd run into someone who didn't know that Asher had died. They would ask, "How's Asher?" and I would think to myself, *"Well, he's great... but I'm not!"*

The first time I drove to town alone, eight weeks after Asher's death, I remember the feeling of the emptiness in the backseat. It felt wrong—Asher was supposed to be there. He was my little buddy. We did everything together.

As you move into the three months following the death, remember the suggestions from the previous section, and consider these as well:

Things To Say:

- **"Tell me about your child,"** or **"Tell me about a favorite memory of your child."**

- **Do share a personal story or memory of the child.** The parents are desperate for any information you may have about their child's life. They may be afraid the world will forget their child or that no one else cared about him. Get them talking about their child. It will be a healing experience for all involved.

It's your job to lovingly meet the parents where they are. Let them lead the conversation or bring up a topic that they want to talk about, and then either listen or speak truth to them.

Things Not To Say:

- "God has a plan," etc. See the previous "Things Not To Say" section—they all still apply.

Things To Do:

- **Share pictures of the child the parents may not have seen.** As with stories and memories, the parents love seeing new pictures of their child. It will mean a lot to them.
- **Know that it doesn't end after the funeral.** In fact, after the funeral may be when the parents enter a new stage of shock. They will be in a pit of despair, especially since their grief will continue as everyone else goes about their normal lives. The funeral may

provide closure for many friends and family members, but it might not for the parents.
- **Enter the parents' bubble.** Lovingly offer to take the parents somewhere, and don't be hurt or offended if they say no. Keep offering. If you are persistent, you can help get them re-introduced to the outside world.

Things Not To Do:

- **Do not assume they're "over it."** They're not—in fact, at three months, a new kind of shock is just starting to set in. Love never dies, and the parents will never "get over" the devastating loss of their child.
- **At the funeral, do not ask the parents to commit to anything, schedule an event, or make a meaningful decision.** People do not make smart decisions and commitments when they are in shock. If you need to schedule something, say, "We'll take care of this later."

As time wore on to four or five months, the shock was wearing off and we began to feel the true pain of the reality of a life without Asher. In a way, the shock had been protecting us. As reality set in, we began to wonder: *why did my life get ripped to shreds while everyone else gets to lead a normal, happy life?* And *how will we ever be happy again when our little boy has been torn from our arms?*

the walk

Red Flags

It's honestly hard to tell what a red flag is in the first few months following a loss. After the death of a child, the parents may not care about anything. They may tell you that they want to die so they can be with their child again. They might isolate themselves in a way that you think is unhealthy. They may feel intense pain for weeks or months on end. Their sense of humor might suddenly change or become very dark. But *these feelings can be completely normal.*

So it's challenging to say when something is a red flag and when it's not. This is why it's important for you to be present in the lives of the parents. As a member of the family unit, you know them best.

If you think the couple would benefit from a retreat, wait until it's been at least three months since the child's death, and then lovingly encourage them to look into something that would fit their needs and situation. Don't push too hard, but do let them know that you love them, and that you want to help them find the resources available.

7
ongoing

However long you think it should take to grieve a loss, multiply it by at least five for a child. As we mentioned in chapter three, parents are considered "newly bereaved" for *five to seven years* after the death of their child. "Newly bereaved" means it feels like the loss happened yesterday.

So after the initial storm is over, after the phone calls and house visits stop and the freezer is no longer full of casseroles, the couple will still need your help and support. Be patient with them as they learn their "new normal." Remember, they are moving bravely forward into a life without their beloved child.

The Firsts

The "firsts" are a big deal for the couple. The first Christmas without their child will be nothing like the Christmas before. The same is true of the first Thanksgiving, the first Easter, the child's next birthday, and the days leading up to them.

Do you have an annual celebration or get-together for any of these holidays? Please be aware that the parents may not wish to participate for the first year or two after the death of their child. They are not being rude, and they are not breaking tradition to spite you. And it's not that they don't want to spend time with you. In fact, it's not about you at all.

For the parents, the firsts are incredibly difficult. Don't be alarmed or offended if they skip your Thanksgiving meal or don't show up on Christmas Eve. Extend grace to the grieving parents, and do not pressure or guilt them into attending. They love you and they miss you, but they may not be able to handle a gathering. And that's okay.

This happened to us for our first Thanksgiving. We were invited to the annual family get-together, but the thought of being around that much family without Asher was overwhelming. It wasn't that we didn't love our family, or that we didn't think we needed them. It was just something we could not handle at that time. So we turned down the invitation and ate pizza with our neighbors instead. It was hard to recognize that it was a holiday and we were missing a very important piece of our family.

So if this happens within your family unit, do not judge, pressure, guilt, or resent the parents. Don't be offended if they leave halfway through Christmas dinner or demand that they stay. Simply extend grace to them, and encourage others to do the same.

Be aware that the "firsts" may extend beyond the first or second year. The parents may struggle with later milestones. For example,

Asher should have started kindergarten last year. Or whenever I attend a wedding, I think, "Asher will never have the chance to get married." As a member of the family unit, be patient and loving, and take positive and healthy actions to help them move through their grief.

Mind and Body

Trauma and loss have a tremendous effect on the human mind and body. For years after the loss of their child, parents may have gaps in their memory. They may have trouble making decisions. They may experience physical pain and stress, and strong emotions such as anger and denial.

These are all normal, but they can be difficult for the family unit to watch. It might also seem like they are taking one step forward and ten steps back in the healing process. This can be painful and frustrating to watch, and hard to understand, but please bear with them. There is no way around the grief. There are no shortcuts. They have to go through it—and it's one of the hardest things they will ever do.

When Denny returned to his job as a phone technician after Asher's death, he struggled because things had changed so much for him, but not for anyone else. There's a gap between where the parent has moved to and where the rest of the world still stands. It was hard for Denny, because he was going through a process of clarifying what really mattered to him.

It was hard for me, too. Asher died on a Monday, and for the first year after Asher's death, every Monday was incredibly painful. Every Monday for a year, I replayed the events of his death in my head, from finding him limp in his crib to leaving the hospital. I couldn't even stand to be in the house from 11:30 in the morning to 1:00 in the afternoon. It was too intense.

So be loving, understanding, and give them grace. The parents are doing the best they can. Share memories, say the child's name often, encourage them, and be present with them. Don't ask them to make any big decisions for at least a year after the child's death. Don't analyze them, rationalize their behavior, or try to force things back to the way they used to be.

Instead, meet them where they are. Know you are not going to be able to fix them. So commit to loving and being patient with them. Grief is a life-long walk, and it's not logical or linear. All you can do is be there with them during their journey.

Stay Attentive

They say time heals all wounds, but Denny and I learned that time is not actually the healer. It may be tempting to look at the couple and think, "Okay, it's been three months, so now the shock should be wearing off and the clarifying pain should begin." Grieving is not a precise science, and everyone is different. You cannot expect the couple to heal according to schedule.

Instead of thinking about healing and grieving in chunks of time, think of it as a walk. The couple is moving from point A

ongoing

(grief) to point B (healing), but they're not walking the path at a set speed or schedule. And in fact, as we talked about earlier, the mother and father might be on different paths themselves. There might be pitfalls along the way, or detours, or one (or both) of the parents might even circle back and start the path all over again from the beginning.

As a member of the family unit, you can be attuned to where the parents are on their path and how they are walking it. They might stumble into a ditch on the first anniversary of their child's death, or take multiple steps forward after a retreat. These are all normal.

Check in with the couple and keep a vague idea of their schedule in mind (though don't stalk them, "helicopter parent" them, or obsess over every detail of their lives). As you keep a loving eye on them, there are a few key things you can be attentive of:

- **Are they in community?** It is important that the parents stay connected with other people, especially the family unit. It's normal for the couple to want some isolation at first (especially during firsts and holidays), but if they have shut themselves off completely, this may be a red flag.
- **What are they seeking?** The couple should be actively seeking something. It might be outward help, healing, memories or photos of their child, peace, companionship, or a retreat, but they should be seeking *something*. If they're not, though, *it is not your responsibility to make them want anything*. It has to come from a desire inside of them.
- **Are they seeing a counselor?** If you can, encourage them to stick with their counselor or attend a support group. Counseling was a

vital part to holding our marriage together, and we would highly recommend it to others.

- **Are they going to church?** It's common for parents to question their faith after the death of their child. What they have been through has stripped them to their core. Be patient with them and don't pass judgement on where they stand with God. If you are a person of faith, the main thing you can do is listen to where they are in that area of their life and be a positive loving source of truth. Encourage them in this journey and invite them to attend church with you.
- **Are they continuing along their path—or have they stopped?** Walking through grief is the hardest thing on the planet. As you watch the parents walk the path of grief, you might see them stop, pause, or even retrace their steps every once in awhile. That's normal. But if they stop completely for a long period of time, or close themselves off to methods that were helping and healing them before, it might be a red flag. They need to keep moving forward, even if the steps are tiny. Keeping their momentum means they will find the freedom to keep moving and the strength to keep going.
- **How are they speaking about their child?** The words the parents use to talk about their child are important. They can help you evaluate where they are on the path of grief. You might have noticed that throughout this book, we have been using the "d-words" (dead, died, death) a lot. It's not because we like the d-words. They're painful, final, and hard to say. It's tempting to use softer words and say the child "passed", "passed away", "went

to his heavenly home", or "moved on". But those softer terms can indicate that the parents have not yet fully accepted their child's death. So if a child died five years ago and the mother still can't say the word "died", it may indicate that she might need help moving forward.

If the parents are doing at least a couple of the above things, then they are moving forward, even if it feels slow. But complete isolation or a lack of activity is a concern. They may have no idea how to move forward. But that's what community, counseling, retreats, church, and family are for.

Please remember, you can't make the parents want to move forward and take action, but you can encourage them and lovingly guide them to the next step on their path. Remember, too, that one hopeless or difficult day does not mean they will be hopeless forever. People will have good days and bad days. That's why it's important for you to make the commitment to be attentive and keep an eye on how they're doing over a long period of time. It's the only way you will know if they are actually making progress.

The Vision of Healing

Sometimes, people ask us, "What is your life like now that you're on the other side of loss?" Five years after Asher's death, Denny and I are still learning new things every day. We will probably continue learning and discovering for the rest of our lives. During the past five years, we have had to learn to navigate our family's "new normal", walking down the path and opening up doors of discovery along the way.

As we've moved forward, we have had to open and walk through door after door. Some of these doors have taken a lot of courage to walk through. Sometimes it's a challenge to even walk *toward* the door, and sometimes we've had to walk through the same door 17 times. But it is only possible to heal if you walk through the doors. Healing isn't a destination but a journey. It's a walk we've committed to taking with each other.

The memories help, though dealing with them is not always easy. One of the things we have learned during our own walk is that the way we respond to memories can have an effect on the doors we are able to walk through. At the end of the day, the beautiful thing about memories is that they're there whether we can talk about them or not—no one can take them away from us.

Day to day, Denny and I are thriving and are experiencing great joy in our life. It's taken a lot of work and intentional focus, but the grief has lifted for the most part, and there is not a lot of weight on us. We are more hopeful now than ever before. We still talk about Asher a lot—every day—but it's all positive. He's still very much a part of our family.

Our boys, Elijah and Isaac, know who Asher is and love him. We have never been silent about his death. The fact that they know him brings us great joy. Our home features photographs of Asher, Elijah, and Isaac. One of my favorite pictures was taken when we visited Asher's gravesite on his birthday this year. Elijah and Isaac stood on either side of his plot and kissed his gravestone, which has his picture engraved on it. I loved seeing all of my boys together.

Our family unit is engaged in our "new normal". They have shown us love and acceptance during our walk and we are forever grateful for their support. My niece's and Asher's birthdays are only days apart, and we had always planned to celebrate together. This year, I didn't know it, but my sister got a special cake for Asher. When it came time for cake, the family sang "Happy Birthday" to both my niece and Asher. It was beautiful. My nine-year-old nephew even insisted that Asher's picture be beside him while he ate. "I'm eating my cake with Asher," he told us proudly.

With the help and support of our friends and family, we will heal. The sun will shine again. We *will* see Asher again. And until then, as my sister shared with me:

> *May the road rise up to meet you.*
> *May the wind always be at your back.*
> *May the sun shine warm upon your face;*
> *The rains fall soft upon your fields*
> *And until we meet again,*
> *May God hold you in the palm of His hand.*

conclusion: the walk

The walk from grief to healing is going to be… interesting. It is going to be challenging. It will never, ever be easy. And it won't be anything like what you expect. Society has painted a picture of what it thinks grieving is like, and it is far from the truth.

If you are grieving, whatever you can do today, reach out, seize it, and take a step. It doesn't matter if you walk ten feet or one inch. If that's what you can do today, great! The feeling of hopelessness is real, but it's also temporary. It will begin to fade as you process the events and find the true source of hope.

If you are a member of a family unit watching parents grieve, take to heart what you've read in this book. You can have a powerful effect on those parents, and your first step in helping them is reaching for a resource like this one. So don't fear their hopelessness. Don't fear their progress (or what may seem like the lack of it). Don't push them in the direction you think they should be moving. Don't despair that the walk through grief feels like it's taking forever.

You are doing a good thing by caring about them. Stay present in their life, and be mindful of where they are and where they're going.

Connect With Us

If you found this book helpful or if you'd like additional resources to help your loved ones through their loss and grief, please get in touch with us at (605) 934-2525, or visit http://www.healinghopes.com/. Hope and healing are possible. We would love to help.

about the authors

Denny and Karri Allen, the founders of Healing Hope Ministries, lost their son Asher when he was just 15 months old. They made a difficult decision the day Asher died that put them on a path to surviving and thriving once again.

While dealing with their own grief, they realized that there were very limited resources to help parents deal with the loss of a child. They have found that it has been most helpful and comforting to talk to others who have walked in their shoes.

Soon after this discovery and working through their grief, they felt God calling them to minister to others going through this terrible loss. Healing Hope Ministries, located near Alcester, SD was founded on March 25, 2016.

Many people have been urging Denny and Karri to share their story, so they hope that this book will be an excellent tool to help family and friends of the bereaved to learn how they can best support each other during this great loss.

the walk

Denny and Karri have three other boys—Tyler (Denny's son), Elijah, and Isaac. God has carried the Allen family through many trials, and they are forever grateful for all love and support they've received from wonderful family and friends.

about healing hope ministries

Healing Hope Ministries reaches out to families who have lost a child at any age to any cause of death. Founded by Denny & Karri Allen in 2016, the vision for Healing Hope Ministries is to create a safe and tranquil environment where families can come stay for three to four days. Located on a beautiful acreage near Alcester, SD, they plan to create a "retreat" for families to get away for a while and focus on their loss. It is their heartfelt mission to stand with these hurting parents and show them they can survive and move through this difficult time.

Healing Hope Ministries
605-934-2525
www.healinghopes.com
www.info@healinghopes.com